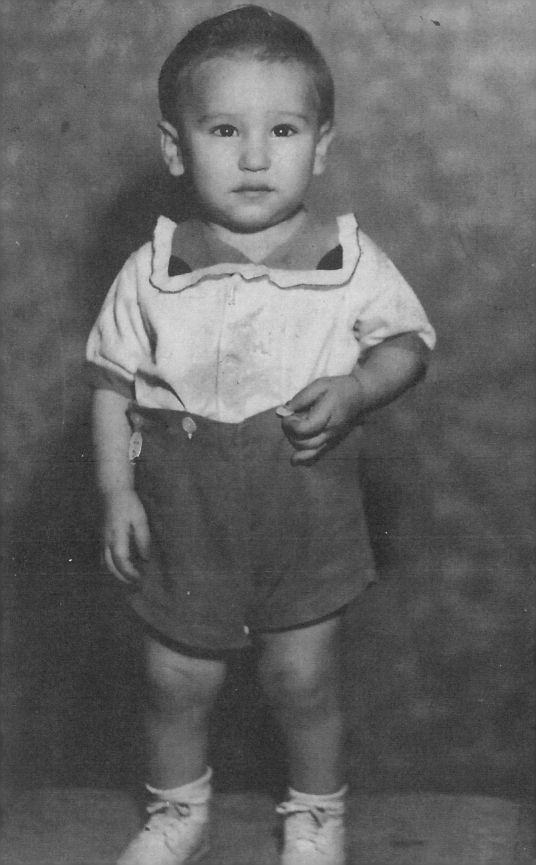

MORE MUSINGS
OF A BARRIO SACK BOY

L. LUIS LOPEZ

LITHIC PRESS
FRUITA, COLORADO

Design & layout by Kyle Harvey

Cover drawing (mixed media) by Richard C. Lopez, author's brother.

Photo of building with broken windows (Santa Fe Railroad Shops) at end of book taken by John J. Lopez, author's brother.

Other photos unknown--probably taken by family members.

MORE MUSINGS OF A BARRIO SACK BOY
L. Luis Lopez
ISBN 978-0-9975017-8-0
Lithic Press

LITHIC PRESS
fine books for an old planet

www.lithicpress.com

To my gramma Petrita whose influence sits so deep in my heart.

*To the 1940 and 1950 residents of the South Broadway neighborhood
in Albuquerque, New Mexico.*

Contents

MORE MUSINGS
OF A BARRIO SACK BOY

The Ditch

Mi gramma didn't talk no English,
she didn't even understand.
"Get water from the ditch,
de la acequia, to water the flowers,"
she told me in Spanish.
The ditch ran in front of our house.
"And don't fall in when you get
it." She had given me a toy
bucket to carry the water
from the ditch to the flowers.
Fifteen trips
it always took to water
the marigolds, roses, and petunias.
"And don't get no water from the
pompe" meaning the faucet. "It
costs too much. Anyway
the ditch has ah, ah, ah,
ah, mas nutrients."
Nutrients?
That's when I found out gramma
was tricking us with no English.

Dementia

When my tía Alicia was eighty-nine
I went to talk with her
but she talked to me like I was
my uncle Silviano
even though I was me, Longene

and

when my gramma Petrita, her sister,
was eighty-eight
I went to talk with her
but she talked to me like I was
my uncle Silviano
even though I was me, Longene

and

when my tía Benita, their sister,
was ninety three
I went to talk with her
but she talked to me like I was
my uncle Silviano
even though I was me, Longene

Hijo!

when I get to be ninety-nine
and
dementia hits me, I hope
that I will think I am me, Longene

and

and not my uncle Silviano

el leñero

el señor Mr. Sedillo
Irene's dad
delivered wood and coal
to our house
every Wednesday afternoon

wood for the stove in the kitchen
for cooking
and
coal for the heater in the living room
where visitors
came to sit and talk

he was never late with the wood
or the coal
he brought it in a wagon
drawn by four horses—I could
always hear them coming
down the street
"anda Prieto, geea Pinto, go Pantalón
dale Posole" then
the creak of wheels
always on time

until el señor Mr. Sedillo bought
a truck, a red one,
to deliver the wood and the coal

he was late on the first day
the battery
a week later the cold didn't
let the engine start

we started running out of wood
out of coal

we started getting worried and mad
looking for wood
in the alley snow
started thinking about the picket fence

then I heard el señor Mr. Sedillo
calling in the cold
"anda Prieto, geea Pinto, go Pantalón,
dale Posole"
the creak of the wheels

Irene said
he was trying to sell the red truck

we were glad
and
he was never late again

El Señor Mr. Watkins the Fuller Brush Man

Mr. Watkins came once a month
on Monday
to sell us brushes and soap and wax
potato peelers
toilet stuff like plungers and mops

he came into the house
put his case on
the floor
and
talked and talked and talked

I kept waiting for him to open
the case
so I could see what new things
he had
but he and mama and gramma and auntie
just talked

finally he winked at me
raised magic
hands
over the case said abra cadabra

snapped the lock
opened it
and right on top of his brushes
and
stuff was a Baby Ruth candy bar which
he said was mine----

then
mama and gramma and auntie bought stuff

The Holy Card Man

The Holy Card Man came to our
house
every Saturday to
show us
plastic saints, rosaries, medals, and candles.

His holy cards were so pretty,
good to hold when praying.

He told stories for each card,
about
St. Francis and birds,
about
St. Ignatius and canons
at Pamplona,
about
St. Isaac Jogues
whose finger nails were pulled
by Indians,
and
about
the other St. Francis who went to China.

About St. Christopher
who
carried the baby Jesus across
a river
in the cold of winter.
He
had him on his shoulders.

It was my favorite holy card story.

He said we should emulate
the saints
so
I asked my dad what emulate meant.

I don't know why
my
gramma got mad, but
she did
when I carried my baby brother
across the ditch
on
my shoulders to emulate St. Christopher.

She told the Holy Card Man
not
to tell me
no more stories
about saints on his Holy Cards.

The Library

Jimmie jumped off his bike,
lifted the paper sack of books
from the basket,
entered the door to the children's
section of the library,
face red from the ride,
the heavy bag,
placed the books on the return desk
so the lady could examine each one,
make sure he would pay pennies
for any overdue.
She stopped at one, looked down at him,
face stern and accusing,
folded back a false cover revealing
a barelegged lovely lady, showy bosom,
one hand holding a pink feather fan,
the other beckoning the reader.
The Case of the Fan Dancer's Horse
by Earl Stanley Gardner, a Perry Mason
mystery. "This goes in the Adult Section.
Who let you check this out?
Did you read it? I can tell by the red
in your face you did. Now you will
have to confess your sin to Father Pat."
Jimmy's face turned more red, but he
said, "It was a good story and there
wasn't no bad stuff in it, not even no
cuss words." Tears welled in his eyes as
he begged, "Can I just confess the cover?"

popsicles

every Thursday evening
after supper
we ate popsicles on the front porch

gramma gave me a quarter
to go to Fred's
to buy five popsicles
but
one day Fred
sent me back to get another nickel

gramma said, "Hijole," but gave me
the nickel

I bought lemon for mama, grape
for Dickie, banana for Jugene,
cherry for me, and strawberry for gramma

we sat and savored coolness in the
cool of the evening,
then gramma said, "Don't throw

the palitos away," said,
"Here's a pencil,
write your names on the palitos

then give them to me," then said,
"Longene, here's a dime,
go buy different kinds
of Kool Aid
before Fred closes the store"

the next Thursday, gramma
didn't give me no money to go
buy no popsicles

but went to the ice box and brought
out frozen Kool Aid cubes
with our names on the palitos,

lemon for mama, grape for Dickie,
banana for Jugene, cherry for me,
and strawberry her favorite for her

the next day Fred at the store asked
me how come gramma didn't
send me for no popsicles no more

I said she said to tell you not to raise
the prices of Kool Aid
or we won't buy nothing no more

El Señor Mr. Cleaners

He picked up and delivered
on Tuesdays
in the morning.
Picked up
gramma's, mama's, and auntie's
coats and dresses,
things
that needed to be dry cleaned.

I didn't understand dry cleaning,
but I wondered
if people could be dry cleaned
so
I wouldn't
have to boil water on the
stove and fill the aluminum tub,
the cajete,
in the kitchen to wash me
and
my brothers every Saturday.

Hombre de Negocios

Tony Pino was a man of business,
neighbors
called him Tony Dimas,
Tony Dimes,
for he was a man of business,
hombre de negocios,
made money by spending.

He did business in the alley
behind the grocery store.

Every Friday when he got his
paycheck,
he bought two bottles of wine,
Mogen David and Thunderbird,
the size with twenty swallows
in each bottle,
one dollar per bottle.

Then he bought two packs
of cigarettes,
Lucky Strikes and Chesterfields,
ten cents per pack,
twenty cigarettes in each.

On Sunday mornings,
day of Our Lord,
he stood in the alley.

Sold wine for ten cents a swallow,
cigarettes for a penny a piece.

Doubled his money
on each bottle
and
on each pack, este hombre de negocios,

Tony Dimas,
man of business,
standing in the alley
behind the grocery store.

El Hombre de Encyclopedias

El hombre de encyclopedias
came to our house when I started
the tenth grade.
He promised
my mom, my dad, and my gramma
that I would end up being
un professor
at the university if they bought
a set of encyclopedias.

They believed him and paid
for them every month
for three years when I would
finish high school
and be ready to go to college.

He showed them a beautiful
book case
that would come with them
for free, and he
told them to keep them in
the front room
so people could see
and
say how much they thought
of the future for their kids.

When I saw the books I couldn't
keep my eyes
from them, so when el hombre
de encyclopedias left,
I started opening the books
and read wherever
there was a picture of something.

By the time I graduated,
I had read
a whole bunch of the books
and
used them for lots of book reports
in English and History and Biology
and other things.

People used to come to our house
to see the books, to see me
reading,
and to say how much my dad, my mom,
and my gramma
cared about my future, said they
were lucky I was
smart
but they didn't know that it was the
books that made me smart.

And you know what?
Years later my dad saw
el hombre de encyclopedias
in Joe's Bar
and said that I had become
a Doctor of Philosophy
and
was a professor at the university.

El hombre de encyclopedias
didn't remember
nothing about him or what
he
said to him about me
becoming
un professor at the university.

One Potato

Claudio came into the grocery store
but never brought no money
to buy anything

he would walk by the produce bins
and I could see him
steal one potato

I told Ben but he said "what's
one potato, let it go
we won't miss it"
so I let it go every time

one evening I was taking a short cut
through the alley

I saw Claudio with two friends
cooking a potato over a fire
in a trash bin
cooking it on a wire coat hanger

when it was cooked he took his knife
and cut it into three pieces
gave a piece to each friend
then looking at me
said "are you hungry?" cut his piece
in half and offered
it to me with a big smile on his face

I took it and I ate it

I told Ben
and Ben said "what did you learn by taking it?"

Tapen las Tortillas
(Cover the Tortillas)

"Tapen las tortillas" my mama
ordered
out of shame
when I was six
and my anglo friends came to visit.

They made fun of our tortilla sandwiches.

"Tapen las tortillas" my mama
ordered
when I was sixteen
and my anglo friends came to visit.
She was afraid
there wouldn't be any left for supper.

Hot tortillas
with butter had become famous.

el hielero

el hielero delivered blocks
of ice to our house
every Thursday at 11:00 o'clock

he had big muscles which bulged
when he carried the blocks with hooks

young, not married, Moses his name,
worked for his uncle
el señor Mr. Abraham who owned
the ice house two blocks away

we had an ice box with two doors
on top where the ice would fit,
keep meat and milk and other
things cold
in the compartment beneath

my teenage sister
and her two girl cousins
knew what time he came

so

they got real clean,
put on perfume,
and
waited for him to come

so

they could see his muscles
when he carried
each block with big hooks

then they ran to Marian's house
then to Corina's to see him deliver there

one day Moses said,
"you girls must be rich to live
In three houses,
I think I will marry all of you
then
I won't have to deliver ice
for my uncle no more

Basura Economics

The basura pickers came every
Wednesday
so we had to put the basura
in two cans,
one for dry
and one for slop,
dry going to the landfill,
slop going to Mr. Villanueva's pigs

He never had to pay to buy food
for his pigs.
He was happy about that,

but

one day Celso,
who delivered the slop to
Mr. Villanueva
and who was studying economics
in school
got the idea that the neighbors
should charge Mr. Villanueva
a fee
for their slop,
so the neighbors took his advice.

Mr. Villanueva got real mad,
decided to
pass the charge on to Ben
at the butcher shop,
and
Ben getting angry
passed it on to the customers
who
got mad at Ben
but
mostly at Celso's basura economics.

I Didn't Have No Dog

I didn't have no dog when I was little
but my cousin Elsie did
Scraggles
kind of brown, kind of little
visited all the relatives in the neighborhood
every morning
knew where our houses were

once he had puppies so he was really a she

at eight o'clock
she went to gramma's house
yap!
gramma gave her a biscochito

at eight fifteen
she came to my house
yap! yap!
I gave her a piece of tortilla

at eight thirty
she went to Aunt Marian's house
yap! yap! yap!
Marian gave her a little biscuit

at eight forty-five
she went to Mela and Cuco's house
yap! yap! yap! yap!
Cuco gave her half a donut

at nine o'clock
she went to Ben's Grocery
yap! yap! yap! yap! yap!
Ben gave her a slice of bologna

then ARF! she went home to Elsie for breakfast

The Day Eddie Died

On my way to school in fifth grade,
I found Eddie in the street with a hole in
his head.

Someone shot him.

I am not a lover of cats, but I did have
Eddie.
I found him in the street with a hole in his
head.

Someone shot him.

I picked him up, took him to my hiding
place
in the hills on the way to school, and put
him
in a hole I had dug to hide something else.

I covered him with dirt, said a
Hail Mary
though I worried about
praying to a girl to bury a boy.
I said a Hail Mary
because it was the only
one I knew all the way through.

When I finished, I said, "Mary, Mother
of God,

Someone shot him.

See the hole in his head?"

Then I cried and played hooky
from school
for the first time because a lump
in my heart was so heavy.

Someone shot him.

"Mary, Mother of God, please
don't let Eddie have a
hole in his head when he's in heaven.

Wrestling at Tingley

Me and Soso were in Ben's Grocery
talking about the championship match
between Bulldog Pletches and the
Masked Marvel at Tingley Colosseum.

We never had no money to go see
the matches so el viejo Mr. Crosby
used to tell us and he told it good.
The match was going to be on Friday.

Ernie el Rainbow Bread delivery man
heard us talking at the store and
said if we don't have nothing to do
on Friday to meet him at the Colosseum

at exactly 5:30 in front of the delivery
door to help him deliver the buns
for the hotdogs and he would pay us
a little for helping him carry them in.

We were there and he said, "If anybody
asks let me explain that you are my
helpers," so we helped him carry the
hotdog buns in but only he came out.

The next morning we found out that
el viejo Mr. Crosby was sick and didn't
go to the match so we went to his house
to tell him. He said we told it real good.

Gringo Food and Mexican Food

When Tommy and I played at his house and we got
hungry, his mother brought out raw cauliflower
for us to eat—I didn't like its funny taste but ate
it out of respect. Then one day she steamed
the cauliflower and served it with butter. It was
really good. Another time she mashed
them like potatoes and put in garlic—really good.

When Tommy and I played at my house and we got
hungry, my mother brought out a bowl of pinto beans
for us to eat—Tommy didn't like the taste
but ate out of respect. One day she put in a little
bit of green chili, not too hot, and Tommy said
it was really good. Another time she mashed
them like potatoes, refried them with chili—really good.

Another time Tommy and I were playing with Clyde
at his house, and when we got hungry his mother
brought out a bowl of steamed cauliflower and hot
pinto beans mixed together—it was really, really good.
Clyde's mother was Mexican, his father a gringo.
They always served both Gringo and Mexican food
in their house, and we always ate out of respect.

january moon

in the cold of the moon
Dickie
jumps from his bed
runs
fevered
white briefs only
towards auntie's house two blocks away

I in charge of him
little brother
sick
dad at bar mom at work

Dickie ten me thirteen
worried
try to catch him

til he runs into auntie's house

the moon reminds me
what
la viejita
who lives in the back
at our house
told me

if

the moon shines
on
the palitos,
wood chips behind the woodbox,
they get magic

I look----it is----a sliver
of moon
behind the woodbox

I take a few
run
to auntie's house
put them
in the tea she is making
for Dickie
he likes the smell
drinks some
getting calm
fever going away

so
I ask
can I take him home

she puts a blanket on his shoulders

me
Dickie
walking in the magic of the moon

Cain and Abel

i

At catechism
Sister Benedetta de Paul
told us the story of
Cain and Abel, how Cain
killed his brother.

She told it this way:

"Cain, tiller of soil, why
did you kill
Abel, shepherd of flocks?

Was it anger
because God rejected
your produce of soil,
accepted
Abel's first born of flocks?

You killed your brother.

'Let us go into open country,'
you said,
and there you tilled
the soil with his blood.

You killed the shepherd of flocks."

Sister Benedetta de Paul
stopped
to look for our reactions—
"Thou shalt not kill,"
she finished and dismissed us.

ii

Dickie and I took summer school
classes in art, we
loved to draw, and draw, and draw,
especially the comics.

One day I took my comic strip

to the teacher,
so
did my brother. She said

I didn't draw the feet right
and
said, "Your brother did better."

She gave him a prize.

In my head I wanted to kill
my brother,
'drawer of the feet that are right'
and
in my head the teacher, too.

iii

Who sinned more, Cain, tiller of soil,
or
I, drawer of the feet that are wrong?

after the war (1946)

first time I saw Salvie
sleeves
rolled up past his elbows

couldn't believe it

a long centipede had bitten
mouth and feet
into his left arm leaving a

scar

when he saw me looking
told me
when fighting in the war

soldiers

sent a squadron of centipedes
against
his unit some attaching

to arms

some to bellies some to backs
some
to feet and legs

even

faces . . . see . . . that one on
the back
of Abentino's neck . . . see

which I see and believe Salvie
because
when I broke my hand falling

from

out of the old elm tree
Doctor Rice
put a centipede right below my

left thumb
when . . . when I was asleep
because
see . . . he used a little one

breakfast smiles

in the first grade
I always had smiling visitors
at the breakfast table

the Cream of Wheat Man with his
white hat
or
the Quaker Oats Man with his
black hat

I wondered why they wore those hats

gramma didn't know, nor mama,
and
daddy said it was for their jobs

I wondered could they change hats

Fred at the grocery store said it would
cost too much

the Cream of Wheat Man could wear
the black hat
and
the Quaker Oats Man could wear
the white hat

it would be ok since they were
both smiling

but my brother said, "No, because
I don't
want the Cream of Wheat
to
taste like Oatmeal
and
the Oatmeal
to
taste like Cream of Wheat"

but to be nice

he drew me a picture of the
Oatmeal Man
with
a white hat
and
the Cream of Wheat Man
with
a black hat

and

he made their smiles real big

aquí estoy
(here I am) story 1

Teofilo Trujillo   proud sailor   U.S. Navy
World War II

told us kids story   after story   about   the ocean

not the war

about creatures that live there

like this one

Captain said   Teofilo   take
six sailors   the skiff   check   that little island

but   careful

sea monsters   many kinds   you never know where

we land   island   full of broken wood
ship stuff   everywhere

hungry   we use the wood   make a cooking fire

eat

suddenly the island rises

up   up   up   my mates   sliding
down one side
me
the other   toward the skiff

I grab it

my mates yelling   screaming   being eaten

I get in   pull away   see the island

disappear

a giant   whale   takes   its place
one leg
sticking   out   of its mouth
aquí estoy   here I am   Teofilo Trujillo
sailor
here   to tell you   that's   what happened

aquí estoy
(here I am) story 2

the destroyer would not move   forward
backward   right   left
In calm sea   stormy sea   high waves
low waves
it stayed in one place   immobile   rooted
rooted to this place

the captain said   Teofilo   get in the water
see what's holding the ship
the anchor is up   but something is holding us

I put on my gear   get in   stay close to the ship
so the waves don't toss me
look   around   front   sides   bottom
and
then the back   where   I see   a little fish
six inches
with its teeth biting a tiny part of the rudder

that's what's holding the ship   so still
the tiny fish   holding it   frozen   then
it lets go
the ship tosses   up   down   right   left
me with it
then it bites the rudder again   the ship

freezes

the storm blows over and I am pulled up
to tell my story

the captain says   get back in the water   get
the fish

I get it with a little net but I can't move it up
or down or away from the ship
even though it has let go of the rudder

aquí estoy   here I am   Teofilo Trujillo
sailor
here   to tell you   more   of what happened

I Learned What Horses

I learned what horses belonged
to what cowboys when I was ten.

It only cost a dime for a ticket to the cowboy
double feature
at the Coronado Theater every Saturday afternoon.

A nickel for a popcorn, a nickel for soda pop,
and for an extra nickel two candy bars.

So me, Jugene, Dickie, Soso, and sometimes
Elsie, my cousin who was a girl
and if she was able to buy me a soda pop, went.

I almost always had only a dime so I liked to
take her, but I'm talking about cowboy
horses. I still remember
what horse belonged to what cowboy.

Tom Mix, my favorite cowboy, had two, Blue
and Tony. Johnny Mack Brown had Rebel.

Champion belonged to Gene Autry,
Silver to the Lone Ranger, and Scout to Tonto.

Lash LaRue rode Black Diamond,
Roy Rogers rode Trigger, Gabby Hayes had Eddie.

Dale Evans, Elsie's favorite
because she was a girl, rode Buttermilk.

Remember Zorro? He had Tornado,
and Hopalong Cassidy chased crooks on Topper.

I feel proud that I still remember
what horses belonged to what cowboys.

Can you name their sidekicks?
I already gave you two,

and oh, Elsie, girls don't count as sidekicks.

Waiting

I am waiting for my mother
to get off the bus
from work,
the five-fifteen, which
stops in front of
Fred's Grocery by the Church.

I'm not supposed to cross
the street
because of all the cars.

When she gets off the bus she
always looks for me
standing by the gate to my yard.

She sees me,
she smiles, and today more than
other times
because I have learned to swing
back and forth on the gate.

Curlers

Ben at the store told me
to collect lids
from

sardine cans and to bring
them to the store to
wash

them to put them in a box
by the cash register
near

the bobby pins, so when I filled
the boxes he put two
for

a penny on a sign—so all the
ladies came to buy
some

plus bobby pins on Saturday
to get ready for Mass on
Sunday

Gusto

I love to hear Enrique laugh and laugh because all the
neighbors can hear him!

I told Sara his wife, "Enrique laughs *con tanto gusto,*"
she said, "You mean with great gusto, like in 'gust of wind'."

"No," I said, "*con tanto gusto* like in goose."

And she said, "No, like gust of wind," because he was laughing
in English at Red Skelton. If he was laughing at Cantinflas, then

you could say *con tanto gusto* like in goose. He's laughing in
English, not in Spanish. So now when I hear Enrique laugh,

I remember how Sara corrected me and I don't like to hear
Enrique laugh no more.

Lonely Tree

I was born and raised in this corner
of the yard.
I think I will see the end of my days
lonely,
oh so lonely, lonely.
The other trees are so far away.

Oh, look.
Here comes that kid
who
drove big nails into my smooth bark
so he could
climb up into my branches
and
sit where my trunk parts,
hidden among my thick leaves.

He keeps me company while
he reads
Captain Marvel,
Batman and Robin,
The Shadow,
The Green Lantern,
and
Lone Ranger
comic books while eating
Fig Newtons
and
drinking Royal Crown Cola.

I'm not one to complain,
but
I wish I could ask him to read out loud
so
I don't feel lonely, oh so lonely.

Bridges

When I was little growing up
my gramma told me,

"Be careful on the bridge
when you go to the store or to school
or to church
because it is old
and the ditch is full,
llena de aqua.
It has loose boards
and lots of nails sticking up."

I asked her why people made
bridges out of old wood.

She laughed,
"You are too smart for your pants."
She told my mom, and they
laughed,
and laughed,
then they called my aunt.

I started thinking
of the other bridges in front
of the houses on our block.

Felina's bridge had a railing
so she don't fall in.
She was old and had a cane.
Her bridge was old like ours.

Mr. Loftus made his bridge
with new wood.
He was always fixing it.
I don't know why he didn't
make it so he
wouldn't have to fix it.

Mr. Rodriguez's bridge was big
and
beautiful, and it was blue, and
I wondered where he got the blue wood.

I think he was rich because
he was a mailman
and wore a blue shirt, blue pants,
a blue cap, shiny black shoes.

At the end of our block
Mr. Davis
had a bridge that was older
than ours. It had broken
wood where you walk
and no railings.
He was a hundred years old,

but that's OK because he used
Mr. Rodriguez's bridge
when he went to
church or to the store to get
a can of Prince Albert for his pipe.

My gramma said, "Uncle Willy
is coming to build
us a new bridge
because Mr. Rodriguez
is getting mad
at everybody for crossing his.

When Uncle Willy came,
he got out of his
pickup
winked at me and said,
"Luis, can you
help me build the bridge?
Look!
I have redwood in the truck.

front porch boxing

we put on winter mittens
to box
on the front porch

imagined Joe Louis vs. Billy Conn

me
Dickie
Jugene
Miel
Nacho

all of us boxing

taking turns with the mittens
until
one tore and we boxed
right hand behind
the back
left one up front to punch

granpa watching said Jugene
hit too hard and
anyway he was left handed

so he sent gramma into the kitchen
to get a mitten
for the hot pots
and made
Jugene
box with that on his left hand

when we boxed Jugene was
Joe Louis
the rest of us took turns
being Billy Conn

Billy Conn won because
Joe Louis'
left was like
spanking with a dish towel

Sister of Charity

when I was little I thought the sisters
didn't have no legs
floated when they came and went

had names not one but three or four

Sister Anne Pierre of the Holy Child
Sister Mary Martha of St. Paul
Sister Margaret Regina of the Holy Angels
Sister Theresa Rose of the Sacred Host

pinched faces inside hoodies

Sister Pierre
(I'm using short names)
old face like a día de los muertos skeleton,
Sister Regina
fat queen face with turned up nose,
Sister Mary
kind beautiful big blue eyes,
Sister Theresa Rose
mad at all of us all the time for everything

each with something to keep us in line

Pierre
wooden yard stick on open palm
Regina
bared knuckles on the noggin
Mary
soft voice sweet smile
Theresa Rose
five Hail Marys while
kneeling on pencils in front of class

but back to legs

one day I saw
Theresa Rose kick a soccer ball
from out of bounds
into the net at the end of the field
she yelled goooal and floated away

Dairy Queen 1952

Dairy Queen on Hazeldine
closes for the winter
December 1, every year.
No one in our neighborhood
eats ice cream in winter.
Custom? Health? Superstition?

I figure something could go
wrong with the stomach,
blood, heart, something.

Blame Dad for thinking
this way. Teaches strange
things. "Drink hot water
in the summer. Opens up
pores, cools the body."

Never wear a hat in the winter.
"Makes the head sweat.
When you take it off, quick
cold hurts the thinking brain."
I sort of don't believe him,
but he's my Dad, so I do.

I say to Mr. Rakes at the
drugstore, "I can't have ice
cream in winter."

He says, "Just order a
steaming cup of coffee
every time you
order ice cream—it's a
balance," so I have to
make sure I have enough
money for coffee
when I order ice cream
in the winter. Rakes'
Drugstore is just outside
our neighborhood

El Coco

Tío Popo López kept me in line
with stories about
El Coco

hiding in bushes, in trees,
in bathrooms
looking
for little boys doing bad things
so
he could punish them

with his eyes
one green, one red looking to
put shame in our heads

I was really scared of him
especially
when Tío Popo said he also
hid in confessionals
where you go to tell your
sins to the priest, to
see if you confessed all of
them—I was always

afraid I left one out, afraid
he would know
what I didn't confess, but I was
lucky
because I never saw no green eye
or red eye in the bushes,
in the trees,
or in the bathroom,

but I asked

Tío Popo what El Coco was
looking for me
to do in the bathroom,
and
boy did Tío Popo get red trying to
explain

especial

come and eat mi tía's sopapillas
puffy hot with honey
she makes them
especial

you need to eat mi tía's tortillas
buttered hot mantequilla
she makes them
especial

come and eat mi tía's empanadas
hot filled with apricot
she makes them
especial

you need to eat mi tía's tamales
pork hot in husk and masa
she makes them
especial

but don't drink a cup of her café
luke warm grainy bitter
not even
cream and sugar can save it
for she makes it
no especial

My Bicicleta

My bicicleta had three speeds
before the invention of handle bar
gears . . . pump, pump harder, and coast.

Pump for level land,
pump harder for going uphill,
and coast for downhill.

I used to ride my brother Dickie
on the handle bars sitting face away,
and sometime my cousin Jugene

his heels on the back axle, hands
holding on to the seat
me standing and pumping the pedals,

and we never wrecked, but we
couldn't go up hill,
so we never coasted downhill.

One day we wanted to see if we could
drink soda pop
while we were all on the bicicleta,

Dickie drinking Royal Crown Cola,
Jugene a Coca Cola,
and me a Nesbit Grape Soda.

Dickie could, Jugene could, but I
couldn't hold the handle bars with
just one hand, so Jugene let go

of the seat and held the grape Soda
to my mouth
and my sister ran along side of us

taking pictures with her plastic camera,
and we made it all the way to
finishing the soda pops without wrecking.

Manitas y Maleta

Modesto y Melchior knocked on our front door,
always looking for work.

We called Modesto "manitas" cause he could
fix anything with his hands.

We called Melchior "maleta" cause he always
carried tools in a canvas bag:

screwdriver, pliers, hammer, hand saw, tape
measure, stuff he didn't know

how, where, or when to use, but Manitas
did. They were brothers. Maleta was

a little touched in the head. Manitas brilliant
jack of all trades. They made their living

house to house for there was always something
to fix that people couldn't fix.

I guess you could say Maleta was a Gabby Hays
or Sancho Panza to Manitas—they worked

so well together. Mom led them into the
bathroom where Maleta handed Manitas

each tool he needed to fix the toilet that
wouldn't flush, the shower that wouldn't

shower, and the sink that didn't drain.
When they finished, Mom took them to the

Kitchen, poured each of them a cup of coffee.
Manitas sat until Maleta sprinkled sugar, poured

milk then handed him a spoon to stir while he
poured milk sprinkled sugar and stirred his own.

Red Herring

My Speech teacher, baseball coach,
study hall monitor,
all Dr. Orlando Smith.
He let us call him Dr. Coach,
even when he was teaching us debate,
said, "Watch for a red herring,
recognize it, don't use it."
Before he could explain, I raised
my hand, asked,
"Who does Red Herring play for?"
Is he like Red Schoendist,
second base for the St. Louis Cardinals?"
Dr. Coach broke out laughing,
his face turning red.
"Red herring is not a guy,
not a baseball player. Red herring is
a type of argument like when
you ask me
about my Border Collie when
I ask you
for your homework."
The class started laughing. My
turn to turn
Red! Red! Red! Red! Red! Red!

Hitting Us

Hijo! I got mad at mama when she hit me with the belt
for something Dickie did. I heard him laughing.
She said she was going to tell daddy when he got home
from work and Hijo! She did. So I went to the yard to get
a big rock from the ground because I knew to get them
back was to break the lectricity glass that has a round
thing that goes round to measure the lectricity we use,
and Hijo! I did. I threw it with the rock and broke all
the lectricity. It went off in the whole house so they
couldn't hear the rancheras on the radio no more, even
in my gramma's part of the house, and they had to call
the lectrician to come fix it. I told them I didn't do it,
that Dickie did it, and so he got hit by mama, and then
by daddy too. Gramma came out of the house with
her broom, her escoba, and started hitting me because
she said she saw me break the lectricity with a big rock.
And, Hijole, Dickie went behind the garage to laugh.
My cousin Jugene was walking by and started laughing.
Gramma heard him and said, "Why do you laugh?"
and hit him on his bottom with the broom, her escoba.

haughty hero

three minutes before three
Johnny
slides
out of his desk,
walks
to the front of the classroom,
takes
the handbell
from its cushioned shelf,
grabs
its tongue,
tiptoes
into the hall
then into the yard,
where
at just the right moment
runs
like a maniac
clang,
clang, clang,
clang, clang, clang,
clang, clang, clang, clang,
then
CLANG
by the principal's office,
grabs
the tongue,
walks,
haughty hero,
back to the classroom,
bell back
on the cushioned shelf.

L. Luis Lopez is a professor emeritus from Colorado Mesa University. He is the author of four books of poetry, *Musings of a Barrio Sack Boy* (2000; Writers Digest Award), *A Painting of Sand* (2000), *Each Month I Sing* (2008; American Book Award and first place in poetry from CIPA), and *Andromeda to Vulpecula: 88 Constellation Poems* (2014). He has also been published in numerous literary magazines.